Bruce Berr

AT THE SEASHORE
VOLUME 2

Notes from the Publisher

Composers In Focus is a series of original piano collections celebrating the creative artistry of contemporary composers. It is through the work of these composers that the piano teaching repertoire is enlarged and enhanced.

It is my hope that students, teachers, and all others who experience this music will be enriched and inspired.

Frank J Hackinson

Frank J. Hackinson, Publisher

Notes from the Composer

These pieces allow the early-level pianist the opportunity to play music that expresses feelings and experiences inspired by trips to the seashore, or perhaps a lakeside beach. A variety of styles is represented—some are introspective and dreamy, others are quick and snappy. These pieces are slightly more advanced technically and more sophisticated musically than those found in Volume 1 of this set.

As you master the mechanics of each piece and desire to bring higher levels of expression to the music, ask yourself: What does the title mean? What images come to mind? What are the clues in the score? If each piece were a person, what kind of personality would it have? Are my musical gestures bold enough to communicate effectively?

The seashore presents us with wonderful opportunities for exploration and fun, as well as great natural beauty. I hope this collection inspires you to appreciate it even more!

Best wishes,

Bruce Berr

Bruce Berr

Contents

In fond memory of Richard Chronister

Wispy Clouds

Bruce Berr

Drifting along playfully (♩. = ca. 44)

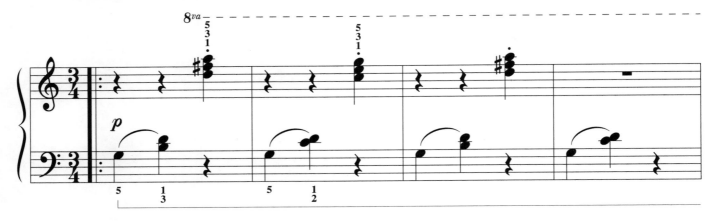

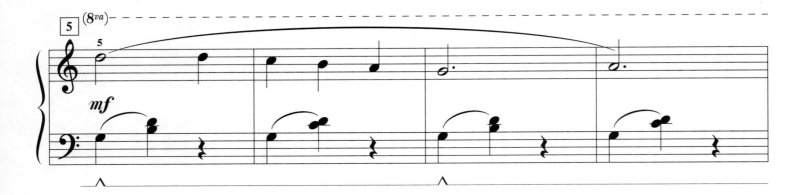

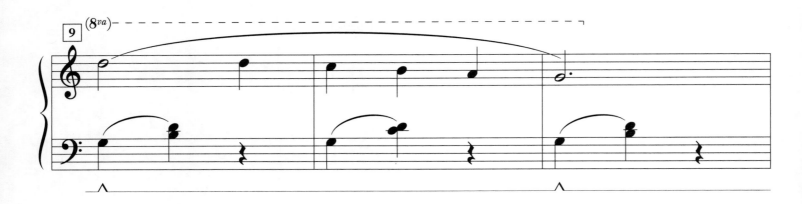

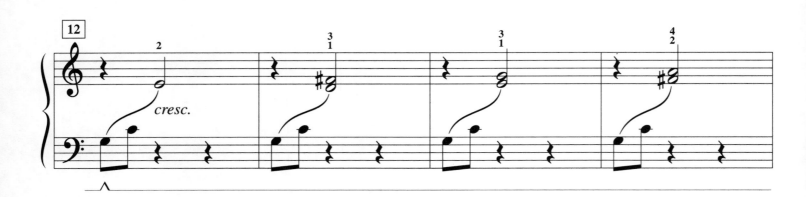

The Distant Shore

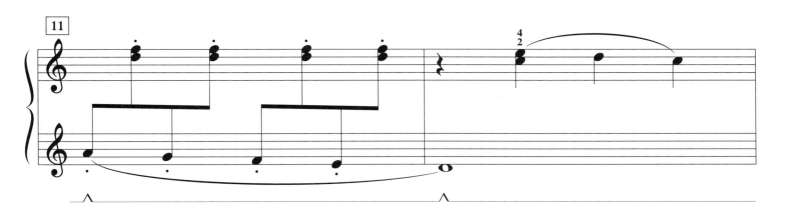

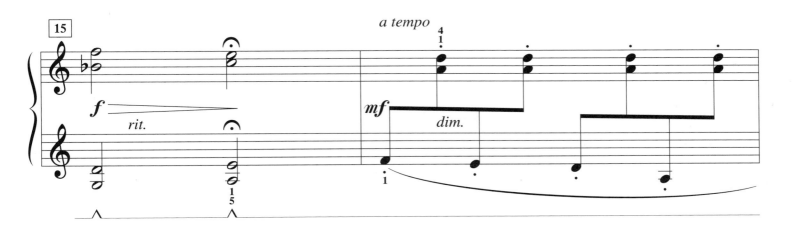

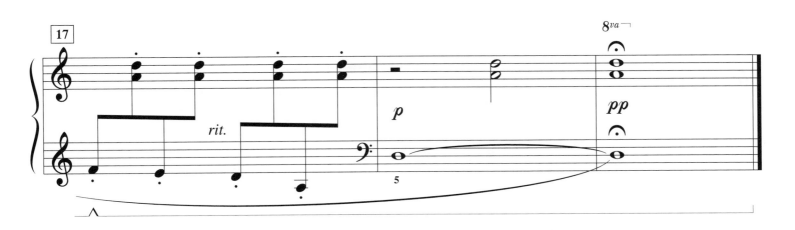

Skating on the Boardwalk

Scooting along (♩ = ca. 100)

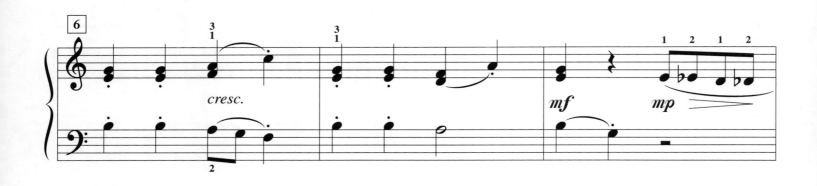

9

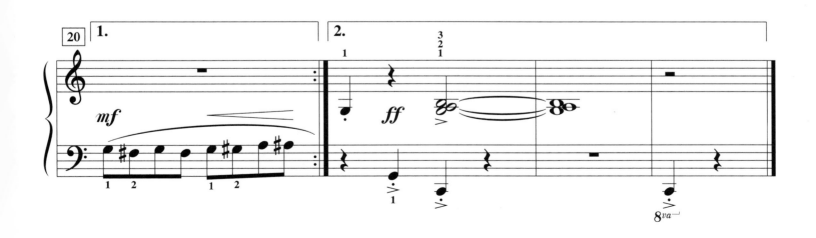

FF1277

Playful Dolphins

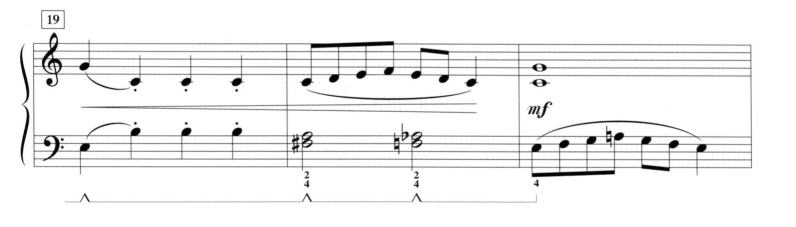

Medieval Sand Castle

13

FF1277

Playing Tag

With energy ($\quad$ = ca. 100)

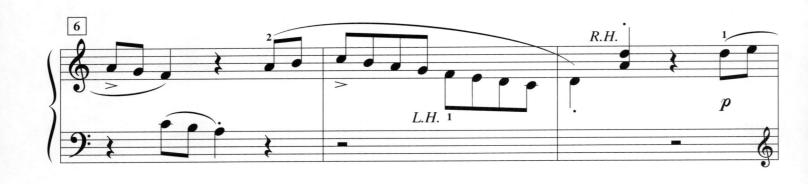

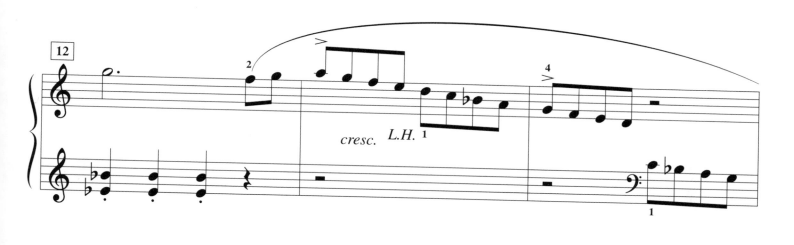

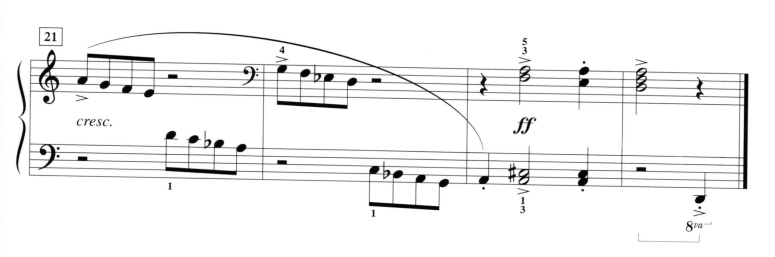

16

Going Home

FF1277

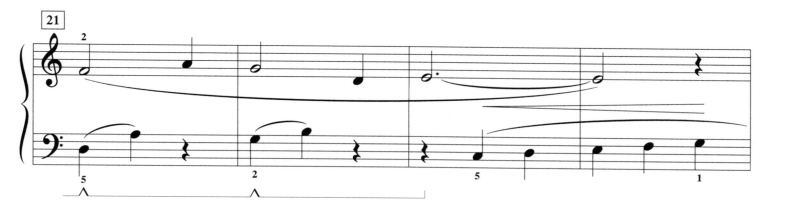